Marie of Guise: Regent of Scotland

A Tudor Times Insight

By Tudor Times

Published by Tudor Times Ltd

Tudor Times Insights

Tudor Times Insights are books collating articles from our website www.tudortimes.co.uk which is a repository for a wide variety of information about the Tudor and Stewart period 1485 – 1625. There you can find material on People, Places, Daily Life, Military & Warfare, Politics & Economics and Religion. The site has a Book Review section, with author interviews and a book club. It also features comprehensive family trees, and a 'What's On' event list with information about forthcoming activities relevant to the Tudors and Stewarts.

Titles in the Series

Profiles

People

Politics & Economy

Contents

Marie of Guise: Regent of Scotland

Introduction

Marie of Guise was a French noblewoman who became Queen Consort of Scotland. Through her determination and political skill she managed to protect her daughter, Queen of Scots at eight days old, from the aggressive policy of the Queen's great-uncle, Henry VIII, who sought to annex Scotland. Finally achieving the position of Regent, she tried to steer a moderate course through the increasingly polarised religious factions, but died in the middle of a rebellion by the Protestant Lords.

Part 5 contains Marie of Guise's Life Story and additional articles about her, looking at different aspects of her life. Marie of Guise protected the inheritance of her daughter, Mary, Queen of Scots, and promoted the Auld Alliance between Scotland and France. She spent her youth in France, before arriving in Scotland aged about twenty-three, to be the second wife of James V. Marie travelled extensively in Lowland Scotland to carry out her functions, first as Queen Consort, then as Regent.

Family Tree

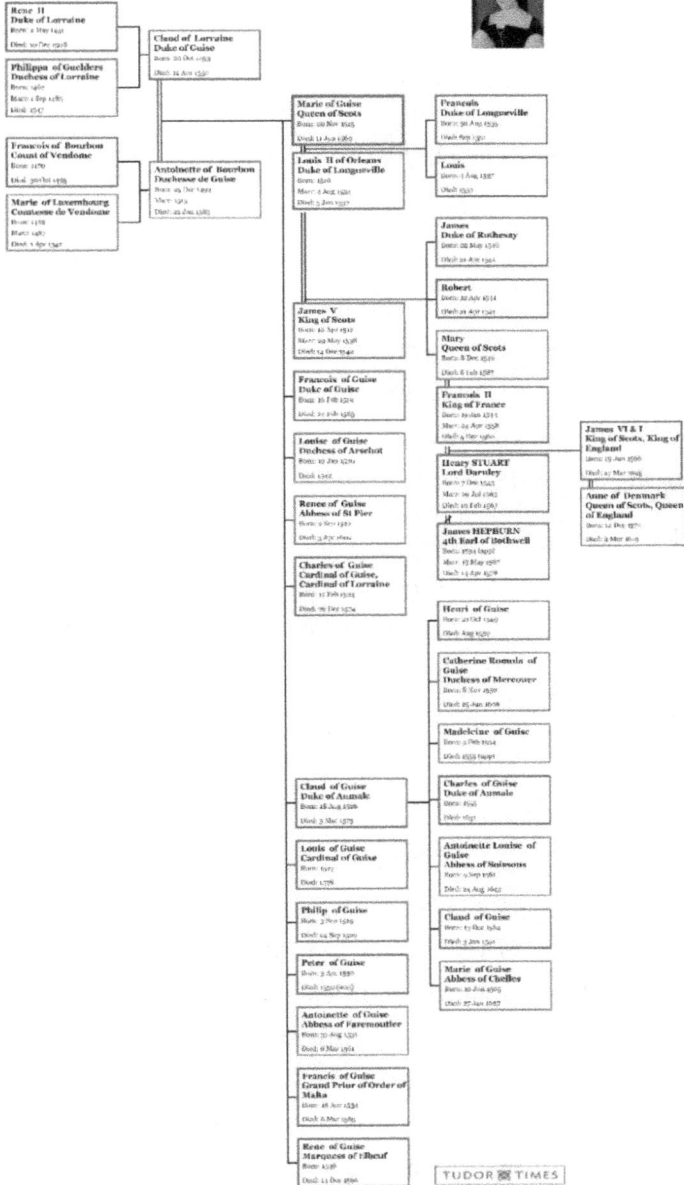

Marie of Guise
Queen of Scots

- René II / Duke of Lorraine / Born: 2 May 1451 / Died: 10 Dec 1508
- Philippa of Guelders / Duchess of Lorraine / Born: 1462 / Died: 1547

→ Claud of Lorraine / Duke of Guise / Born: 20 Oct 1496 / Died: 12 Apr 1550

- François of Bourbon / Count of Vendôme / Born: 1470 / Died: 30 Oct 1495
- Marie of Luxembourg / Comtesse de Vendôme / Born: 1472 / Died: 1 Apr 1547

→ Antoinette of Bourbon / Duchesse de Guise / Born: 25 Dec 1493 / Died: 22 Jan 1583

Children of Claud of Lorraine and Antoinette of Bourbon:

- **Marie of Guise / Queen of Scots** / Born: 20 Nov 1515 / Died: 11 Jun 1560
  - m. **François / Duke of Longueville** / Born: 30 Aug 1535 / Died: Sep 1551
    - **Louis** / Born: 1 Aug 1537 / Died: 1537
  - m. **Louis II of Orléans / Duke of Longueville** / Born: 1510 / Died: 9 Jun 1537
    - **James / Duke of Rothesay** / Born: 22 May 1540 / Died: 22 Apr 1541
    - **Robert** / Born: 12 Apr 1541 / Died: 22 Apr 1541
    - **Mary / Queen of Scots** / Born: 8 Dec 1542 / Died: 8 Feb 1587
      - m. **François II / King of France** / Born: 19 Jan 1544 / Died: 5 Dec 1560
      - m. **Henry STUART / Lord Darnley** / Born: 7 Dec 1545 / Died: 10 Feb 1567
        - **James VI & I / King of Scots, King of England** / Born: 19 Jun 1566 / Died: 27 Mar 1625
          - m. **Anne of Denmark / Queen of Scots, Queen of England** / Born: 12 Dec 1574 / Died: 2 Mar 1619
      - m. **James HEPBURN / 4th Earl of Bothwell** / Born: 1534 (1535) / Died: 14 Apr 1578

- **James V / King of Scots** / Born: 10 Apr 1512 / Married 18 May 1538 / Died: 14 Dec 1542

- **François of Guise / Duke of Guise** / Born: 16 Feb 1519 / Died: 24 Feb 1563

- **Louise of Guise / Duchess of Arschot** / Born: 10 Jan 1520 / Died: 1542

- **Renée of Guise / Abbess of St Pier** / Born: 2 Sep 1522 / Died: 1 Apr 1602

- **Charles of Guise / Cardinal of Guise, Cardinal of Lorraine** / Born: 17 Feb 1524 / Died: 26 Dec 1574

- **Claud of Guise / Duke of Aumale** / Born: 18 Aug 1526 / Died: 3 Mar 1573
  - **Henri of Guise** / Born: 21 Oct 1549 / Died: Aug 1559
  - **Catherine Romola of Guise / Duchess of Mercoeur** / Born: 8 Nov 1552 / Died: 25 Jan 1596
  - **Madeleine of Guise** / Born: 5 Feb 1554 / Died: 1555 (1561)
  - **Charles of Guise / Duke of Aumale** / Born: 1556 / Died: 1631
  - **Antoinette Louise of Guise / Abbess of Soissons** / Born: 2 Sep 1561 / Died: 24 Aug 1643
  - **Claud of Guise** / Born: 17 Oct 1564 / Died: 3 Jan 1591
  - **Marie of Guise / Abbess of Chelles** / Born: 10 Jun 1565 / Died: 27 Jan 1627

- **Louis of Guise / Cardinal of Guise** / Born: 1527 / Died: 1578

- **Philip of Guise** / Born: 3 Nov 1529 / Died: 24 Sep 1529

- **Peter of Guise** / Born: 3 Apr 1530 / Died: 1530 (1531)

- **Antoinette of Guise / Abbess of Faremoutier** / Born: 30 Aug 1531 / Died: 6 Mar 1561

- **Francis of Guise / Grand Prior of Order of Malta** / Born: 18 Apr 1534 / Died: 6 Mar 1563

- **René of Guise / Marquess of Elbeuf** / Born: 1536 / Died: 13 Oct 1566

Marie of Guise's Life Story

Chapter 1: Early Life (1515 – 1531)

Marie of Guise, or Marie/Mary of Lorraine as she is sometimes known, was the eldest of the twelve children of Claud of Lorraine, Duke of Guise. The Dukes of Lorraine (who liked to refer to themselves as Kings of Sicily) ruled an independent territory within the Holy Roman Empire, the remnant of Carolingian province of Lotharingia. Lorraine was situated to the north-east of France and remained independent of its neighbour until the mid-eighteenth century.

Marie's father was the second son of Rene II of Lorraine, and became a naturalised Frenchman. He was a close friend of Francois I of France, fighting for him at the Battle of Marignano, and was granted the Duchy of Guise, although, as the cadet branch of a sovereign house, the Guise family outranked many of the French nobility – a situation which, together with Francois I's continued favour, caused some resentment at the French court. Marie's mother was Antoinette of Bourbon, daughter of a branch of the French royal family.

Marie spent her early childhood at the Guise chateau of Joinville, before being sent to the Poor Clare convent of Pont-au-Mousson, where her grandmother, Philippa of Guelders, Duchess of Lorraine, had retired in 1519. Marie was sent to the convent, with the intention that she, too, would enter the religious life. The life of a Poor Clare was ascetic in the extreme, including sleeping on straw mattresses as well as undertaking all of the manual work of the convent. The nuns cooked, cleaned and managed their gardens themselves as well as undertaking their religious duties. Marie is presumed to have done likewise.

Marie's education at the convent was designed to fit her for the role of Abbess, however in 1529, her uncle, Antoine II, Duke of Lorraine, decided there was a better use for his attractive and witty niece than being a nun. Following the Peasant Risings in Germany, precipitated by the early Lutheran movement, Lorraine, too faced internal insurrection.

The family needed to increase its strength and influence and a marriage for his niece to a peer of France (or even, if Antoine were lucky, one of the King's sons) would be valuable. Marie was taken to the Lorraine court at Nancy where the Duchess, Renee of Bourbon, taught her more worldly skills than those that had been deemed suitable for a contemplative nun. On 5 March 1531, Marie was presented to King François, and his new Queen, Eleanor of Austria. Marie was naturally charming and attractive, and won the approval of François I (not hard for a pretty girl to do, as he was a notorious lecher). She also developed friendships with his daughters, Madeleine and Marguerite.

Chapter 2: First Marriage (1531 – 1537)

It is likely that Marie spent the period 1531 – 1534 at the French Court. In 1534, François I personally involved himself in arranging her marriage to Louis d'Orleans, Duke of Longueville and Hereditary Grand Chamberlain of France. Marie's father, who seems to have been rather close-fisted as far as his daughters were concerned, refused to give Marie a sufficient dowry. François stepped in to make up the 80,000 livres offered by Claud, to the required 120,000.

The Longueville estates were in the north and west of France, centred round Normandy and the Loire, and Marie received the chateau of Chateaudun as her jointure. The whole of the French Court was present for the ceremony at the Louvre on 4th August 1534. The bride was 18, and the groom some five years older.

Marie and Louis' first son, Francois, was born 30th October 1535 at Amiens. Later letters from Marie's own mother, Antoinette of Bourbon, hint at some discord between Marie and her mother-in-law, Jeanne de Hochberg, who was Countess of Neuchatel in her own right, but whether there was anything more substantial than the not-unusual mother-in-law difficulties, cannot be ascertained.

On 1st January 1537 Marie attended the French court for the wedding of the Princess Madeleine to James V of Scotland. Madeleine's father had been reluctant to agree to the match as the princess was consumptive and the damp climate of Scotland was unlikely to suit her. James strongly desired the match to boost his ability to resist his menacing uncle, Henry VIII of England, and also seems to have become fond of Madeleine herself. Madeleine, too, wanted the match – apparently saying she wished to be a queen before she died. The match was celebrated at Notre Dame with Marie in attendance.

In the spring of 1537, Marie returned to Chateaudun, her husband being due to follow her. Unfortunately, Louis fell ill, perhaps with chicken pox, and died at Rouen on 9th June 1537. His last letter to his wife closes with the words

'I shall say no more...praying God to give you always whatever you desire, your good husband and friend, Louis.'

Marie was pregnant and on 4th August 1537 (her third wedding anniversary) gave birth to a second son, Louis, who died within months.

Chapter 3: Marriage Negotiations

1537 was a year of bad news for Marie. She heard in July that her friend, Madeleine, Queen of Scots, had died. Her first reaction is likely to have been sorrow, followed by dismay when she heard that James, still without a legitimate heir, was looking for a replacement bride, preferably of equal prestige to Madeleine. King François had other plans for his daughter Marguerite (who became Duchess of Savoy), and decided that Marie would make a suitable Queen of Scots. Marie did not want to leave her home and her son and initially refused. François pressed her and James wrote, pleading his suit, personally.

If Marie really did not want to be Queen of Scots, an alternative was soon available. Henry VIII of England, widowed by the death of his third wife Jane Seymour in childbed, was in the market for a fourth. He was eager for a match with either France or the Empire to re-establish himself as a member of the European royal circle after the rift caused by his casting-off of the Emperor's aunt. Henry was also happy to disrupt any plans James V might have and seized the idea that Marie might be just the wife for him - a widowed mother of sons, who was good looking, and exceptionally tall, seemed ideal.

Marie resisted this idea even more strenuously, apparently saying that although she was tall, her neck was very small. Suddenly, marriage to James looked more appealing. Her father again showed reluctance to provide the dowry expected – the Scots were demanding some 150,000 livres, and initially, Claud suggested that it should be paid from the Longueville estates. This would have defrauded her son, François, of part of his inheritance and Marie refused. Eventually, King François offered 70,000 livres and gouged the remainder from Claud.

The marriage contract was drawn up by Cardinal David Beaton, acting for James, and Marie's father. In return for the dowry, Marie's grant as Queen of Scots was the palace of Falkland; Stirling, Dingwall and

Threave castles; the revenues of the Earldoms of Orkney, Fife, Strathearn and Ross, and the lordships of Galloway, Ardmeneach and The Isles. In the event of James pre-deceasing her, if they had children, she would have one third of the amount of her dowry, or half if there were no children. Marie was also indemnified against responsibility for any of his debts. She would be able to retain this dower, even if she returned to France.

Chapter 4: Queen of Scots

The wedding took place at Chateaudun on 9th May 1538, following the necessary dispensation from the Pope, as the couple were third cousins. The link was the familial connection through the Duchy of Guelders. Marie's grandmother, Philippa of Guelders was niece to Marie of Guelders, wife of James II of Scotland.

For his second marriage, James was represented by his proxy, Robert, Lord Maxwell. The bride's wedding ring contained a single diamond and cost James 300 crowns. Marie was now Queen of Scots.

She set sail in June for her new country, arriving at Balcomie in Fife towards the end of the month, pleasingly free from sea-sickness. Marie and James went through a further marriage ceremony at St Andrew's, before taking a trip, both to show Marie the country, and to let the Scots see their new queen. A formal entry into Edinburgh took place on 16th November 1538, followed by her coronation on 22nd February 1540 at Holyrood Abbey.

Marie and James do not seem to have been very compatible personally. He continued his flagrant womanising, and there are letters from him in which he seems to be brushing aside her requests for him to return home and her fears that he has forgotten her. Whatever they felt about each other, they knew their duty and produced two sons in quick succession – James in May 1540 and Robert in April 1541. Heartbreakingly, both boys died on the same day, 21st April 1541. They were buried in the same tomb as Queen Madeleine.

Whilst Queen, Marie spent much of her time in architectural projects. This was one area of interest that she and James had in common, and significant sums were expended on the refurbishing and updating of Falkland Palace, Linlithgow and Stirling. Marie's knowledge of the beautiful palaces of the Loire must have influenced the design.

There was also frequent correspondence with her mother, in which Antoinette relays family news and reassures Marie as the health of her son, the Duke of Longueville. She tells her daughter that little François was so happy in the company of his grandfather, that he has 'lost some of his naughtiness', and that the two could only part in tears.

In other letters from her son's governess, Mlle Jeanne, François sends messages to his mother typical of any little boy

'I have a pony, now I want a big horse, it is to be black. Madame Grandmere takes me often round her garden.'

Marie also managed to build a relationship with James' difficult mother, Margaret Tudor, the Dowager Queen. Henry VIII's Ambassador recorded Margaret's statement that 'she was well treated and made much of, of the new Queen (Marie)'

Queen Margaret had spent most of her life trying to reconcile the country of her birth with the country of her adoption. Throughout the late 1530s both countries had carried out raids and low level acts of aggression, but Margaret had continued to press for a meeting between James and his uncle, Henry VIII.

Various plans had been drafted but it was not until 1541 that it looked as though years of negotiation might finally bear fruit. Henry believed that James had agreed to meet him at York, whither he was travelling as part of a wider progress to demonstrate royal power following the Pilgrimage of Grace. The Abbey of St Mary at York was refurbished for James and his entourage, and arrangements made for safe-conduct through the north of England. James however, had never made any specific promise and the upshot was that he remained at home. Henry was beyond furious. He felt he had been humiliated by James and he would have his revenge.

Talks continued, but there was no real will on either side for peace. In October 1542 Thomas Howard, 3rd Duke of Norfolk, marched in excess of 10,000 men into Scotland on a spree of burning and looting between Berwick and Kelso, before retiring back into England. Henry also repeated his inflammatory claim that he was Scotland's overlord.

James raised some 15,000 troops and made a counter-attack, although, learning the lesson of his father's death at Flodden, he did not lead his troops personally, but remained close by. Whether through ill-luck or incompetence, the Scots force was annihilated between the rivers Esk and Lyne and well over a thousand Scots were taken prisoner, including the Earls of Cassilis, Glencairn and Lord Maxwell who were sent south to Henry.

To compound the loss, James fell ill, probably with dysentery, and, retreating to Falkland Palace, died on the 14th December 1542. The news of his wife's safe delivery of a child failed to comfort his last hours, as the baby was a girl, named Mary. This week old child was now Queen of Scots.

Chapter 57: Appointment of the Earl of Arran

The politics of the following twenty years in Scotland, and its relationship with England, should be looked at through the prism of the long struggle for dominance in Europe between France and the Hapsburg empire (including Spain from 1519), which began in the 1490s and was not resolved for another two hundred years. Religion became a complicating factor in the 1560s but, although growing in importance, was not the paramount issue (other than for individual fanatics on both sides) in the period up until Marie's death.

Once Scotland was left with a sovereign Queen, the choice of her future husband became a serious matter. If Scotland were forced into a union with England, then this would tend to favour the Hapsburgs as the old Burgundian and Spanish alliances with England were still preferred. If France could retain its Scottish ally, that would continue its traditional strategy of diverting English troops to the Border, and making incursions into France by England, either unilaterally or in support of the Empire, more difficult.

On the death of James V, two factions began to form amongst the Scottish nobles, although the strength and make up of each ebbed and flowed, and the situation was never straightforward. By and large, there was a faction that was pro-English and, in the case of some of the nobles, there was a desire to bring in a measure of Protestant Reformation, which James had firmly rejected. The second group preferred the traditional Auld Alliance with France, and were generally committed to maintaining the Catholic faith. However affiliations were not black and white, and there were Protestants who looked towards France, and Catholics who believed an accord with England was appropriate.

Marie's own allegiance was always primarily to the advancement of her dynasty, through her daughter, the Queen of Scots, and the Guise family in France. There is no reason to suppose that she did not genuinely feel that Scotland would be better protected in alliance with France, but Scottish welfare was not necessarily her primary concern.

On James V's death, the twenty-four year old James Hamilton, Earl of Arran and heir to the throne after the baby Queen Mary, came forward as the likely Regent.   He was the great-grandson of James II.   This immediately caused a dispute, as Cardinal Beaton claimed that James V had appointed a Regency Council consisting of Cardinal Beaton himself, the Earls of Huntly, Murray, Argyll and Arran, perhaps with Marie included.   Arran denounced Beaton's document as a forgery, but agreed to Beaton being named as Chancellor.

The rapprochement was short-lived and Beaton was arrested and sent to Blackness Castle at the end of January 1543.   Arran was formally appointed Governor by the Estates of Scotland on 3rd March 1543 and Marie confirmed her allegiance to him on the following day.

One of Arran's first acts, rather surprisingly, was to write to the English general, Lord Lisle, that he hoped *to put some reformation in the state of the kirk in the realm.*' The Catholic Church in Scotland was in no better state than anywhere else in Europe, with many of its clergy leading blatantly immoral lives and using church lands and benefices to line their own pockets.   In a country poorer than most, the scale of corruption was even more distasteful.   One of Arran's early reforms was to allow the reading of the Bible in the vernacular from March 1543.   He did not go so far down the road of Protestantism as to reject the Pope entirely, and by May was requesting papal protection and aid against England, whilst still treating with Henry for an alliance.

Chapter 5: Rivals for the Regency

Within weeks of James' death, Henry VIII had come up with the splendid notion (in his own view, at any rate) that the little Queen should be married to his son, Edward, and the kingdoms united under their children.   Marie received letters from Charles Brandon, Duke of Suffolk, one of Henry's chief councillors, promoting the scheme of the marriage and saying *'I cannot therefore bot rejoyse and be moste glad to heare tell of your good towardness and conformytie in that bihaulfe'.*

Henry was also working on the lords who had been captured at Solway, and extracting oaths from them that they would support the union. Once they had done so, they were permitted to return to Scotland to add weight to the pro-English faction and were referred to by their new English masters as *'the Assured Lords'*. Arran signed the Treaties of Greenwich, which would give effect to the marriage of Mary, Queen of Scots to Prince Edward. The Treasurer of Scotland, James Kirkcaldy of Grange, ratified the Treaties on Scotland's behalf on 25th August 1543, but by this time the political landscape had changed.

Arran had a rival for the regency in the shape of Matthew Stuart (he had adopted the French spelling), Earl of Lennox. Lennox was the grandson of James III. He had spent much of his life at the French Court and as soldier in Francois I's army and believed that he, rather than Arran, was the heir and ought thus to be Regent. His claim was based on Arran's possible illegitimacy. Lennox hotfooted it to Scotland, arriving at Linlithgow in April of 1543, ostensibly to act in the French interest.

Regardless of who held the regency, Marie was determined to hold on to her daughter physically, whereas the Scots nobles wished her to be delivered up to guardians, who would rotate quarterly in pairs between the Earl Marischal, the Earl of Montrose, Lords Erskine, Ruthven, Livingston, Lindsay, Seton and Calder. In late March or early April of 1543 she received a letter from George Gordon, 4th Earl of Huntley, saying she could not go to Stirling without handing over the Queen. Rather than comply, Marie remained at Linlithgow.

As the summer of 1543 progressed, the Scottish Estates and those opposed to Arran and the pro-English policy grew stronger. Lennox was hoping to improve his cause by marrying Marie and thus securing both the Regency and the guardianship of the Queen.

Marie, whose primary concern was her daughter's safety, sought to play all of the parties off against each other. She made gracious noises to the English Ambassador, Sir Ralph Sadler, and gave him reason to believe she approved of the proposed marriage of Mary and Edward. Sadler was invited to see the baby and told by Marie that

'she knew not throughout the world any marriage could be found so proper, so beneficial and so honourable as this.'

She added, to muddy the waters, that Arran was probably false in his protestations of desiring the match, as, in reality, he wanted the baby queen to marry his own son.

Meanwhile, Marie was giving encouragement to Lennox, allowing him to think that matrimony was a possibility and backed by his men, managed to make the journey from the difficult-to-defend palace of Linlithgow to Stirling, the most formidable fortress in Scotland. Marie and Mary spent the next few years there. Once there, Marie arranged for the coronation of the little girl, which took place on 9th September in the Chapel Royal – a significant date in Scottish history: thirty years to the day from the battle of Flodden.

Even Arran and his supporters, including the Assured Lords, were growing restive under Henry VIII's bullying tactics, and the overwhelming feeling in Scotland was pushing for a renewal of the French alliance. The Estates of Scotland rejected the Treaty of Greenwich on 11th December 1543.

Lennox, too, was playing a double game. François I had finally realised the threat to French interests in Scotland and sent 10,000 crowns, munitions and ships to support Carinal Beaton and Lennox as the leaders of the pro-French party. By the end of October 1543, Lennox was at Dumbarton Castle, whence the French money, together with munitions, the Legate from the Pope, and the French Ambassador had been sent. Lennox, however, refused to hand it over.

Beaton and Marie were appalled at this betrayal and asked Francois to recall Lennox as a *'troubler of the state'*. Queen Marie told the Venetian envoy that she would have preferred the gold to be at *'the bottom of the sea'* rather than that it should fall into Lennox' hands.

In a last ditch attempt to bring the two factions together, a new agreement was arranged between Arran and Lennox, under which Lennox would accept Arran as Governor, but Lennox failed to observe its terms. Arran now moved decisively towards France, and Lennox defected completely to England, marrying Henry VIII's niece, Lady Margaret Douglas, who was also half-aunt to the Queen of Scots.

Chapter 6: War of the Rough Wooing

Henry VIII was beside himself at the rejection of the Treaty of Greenwich and thus began the *'War of the Rough Wooing'*. He would spare neither money nor men to bring Scotland to heel, and sent his brother-in-law, Edward Seymour, Earl of Hertford, to

'Put all to fire and sword, burn Edinburgh town...putting man, woman and child to fire and sword, without exception where any resistance shall be made.'

Hertford did his best to follow orders and wreaked destruction in the lands around Edinburgh, although he could not capture the Castle. Despite this, the Queen of Scots remained safe from her great-uncle, with Marie at Stirling.

By June of 1544, the Scots nobles were sufficiently unimpressed by the performance of Arran for them to consider giving Marie a place in government – presumably counting on her relationship with France as a factor in her suitability. A Convention held at Stirling agreed that she would head a sixteen-man advisory council for Arran.

Beaton, however, remained as the strongest adversary to Arran, although both were now, in theory, committed to resisting England.

Beaton, although not by any means a fanatical man of religion, despite his Cardinalate, had the radical, but popular, Protestant preacher, George Wishart, burnt for heresy. This was probably the single act that would bear most fruit for the Protestant Reformers in Scotland. Wishart's supporters, together with Beaton's political enemies, assassinated Beaton on 28th May 1546 and barricaded themselves in to his castle at St Andrew's, holding Arran's son hostage to prevent reprisals.

In 1547 both Henry VIII of England and François I of France died. This did not, as might have been expected, reduce tensions, rather it increased problems for Scotland as Lord Protector Somerset (Hertford's new title) upped the pressure, and François' heir, Henri II, began to take a serious interest in Scotland.

Before Marie married James V, there had been a rumour that Henri would divorce his wife, Catherine de Medici, to marry Marie – perhaps a warm personal relationship between Henri and Marie is one of the factors in his support of her. One of Henri's first moves was to send a force to relieve Beaton's castle of St Andrew's, which was achieved in six hours by bombardment from French shipping. One of the men captured and sent to the French galleys was John Knox, who was to prove a thorn in Marie's side.

In September 1547, Somerset led a huge force into Scotland. He had received assurances from the pro-English faction, including Lennox, that there would be local support for him, but it did not materialise. Even without this, despite some initial early Scottish success, the Scots were massacred on Saturday, 10th September; thousands cut down as they fled the carnage. The Battle of Pinkie Cleugh was the last, terrible conflict between England and Scotland as independent nations.

Somerset burnt Leith, but did not follow up his victory in any meaningful military way although he occupied land and fortified castles at Roxburghe, Home, Inchcolm, Broughty, Lauder, Haddington, Inchkeith and Dunglass with a view to having a base for further incursion. Simultaneously, he continued to promote the idea of a union between the two countries, designed to appeal to the growing Protestant faction.

Nevertheless, the vast majority of Scots, perhaps encouraged by French pensions, remained resolutely opposed to union, (or as they saw it, subjection), with England. On 16th October a Convention at Edinburgh agreed to ask for French help. In January 1548, Arran and Henri II agreed a new arrangement. Queen Mary would be sent to France to marry the Dauphin, and, in the long term, Mary's children would be kings of both France and Scotland. In the meanwhile, Henri would extend French protection, in the shape of money and men, to Scotland. For this he would also receive the two castles of Dunbar and Blackness.

Arran (who had hoped to marry his own son to the Queen) was mollified by 12,000 livres, a French Duchy (Chatelherault) and promises of the daughter of the Duke of Montpensier for his son. He was to remain Regent until Mary was of age. In addition, the French were to agree that

> 'the realm, laws and liberties thereof (were to be kept) as has been in all kings' times of Scotland bypast and to marry her (Mary) upon no other person but upon the said Dauphin.'

On 16th June 1548, 6,000 French troops arrived to reinforce Scottish strength and try to wrest the fortresses Somerset had grabbed from English control. Marie, together with the Court, travelled to Haddington, where the castle, held by the English, was under siege. The Estates were called to meet in the Abbey. The Earl of Angus carried the crown, the Earl of Argyll, the sceptre and Lord Rothes the sword of Honour. On 7th

July 1548, Arran and the Estates consented to the marriage of Mary to the Dauphin, with the details enshrined in the Treaty of Haddington.

Politically, Marie was delighted with the outcome. Her daughter would be Queen of France as well as of Scots, and the Guise family would be able to increase its influential position in both countries. Personally, it must have been a terrible blow to send her little girl, only five years old, to France without her.

Chapter 7: Diplomatic Visits

During the following years Marie corresponded regularly with her daughter, whilst carefully drawing towards her goal of being declared Regent. Henri II of France, who now declared that he considered *'[Scotland as a] Kingdom in my protection I consider mine'* consulted Marie on everything before presenting any policies to Arran, who was, in effect, rubber-stamping Henri and Marie's plans. As yet, there was no religious discrimination in the policies pursued by France, with both Catholics and Protestants receiving offices and rewards.

England continued to make war-like noises, but Somerset's hands were tied, first by the Western Rebellion of 1549 which absorbed money and men originally destined for Scotland, and then by the outbreak of hostilities with France over the town of Boulogne, captured by Henry VIII in 1546. A peace between France and England was eventually brokered in 1549, with Scotland represented by the French envoys. There was still contention over the fate of the fortresses controlled by the English, but, eventually a final treaty was agreed between Scotland and England at Norham in June 1551.

In 1550, Marie decided to pay a visit to France. Henri II made a personal request for a safe-conduct for herself and her entourage, and any French galley sent to fetch her, to land in an English port, if necessary, and be treated as a friend. An additional request for her horses to travel overland was also requested. Edward VI's council granted the safe-conducts, for Marie and her train, and up to 100 horses, and 140 men to '*convey*' the animals.

Accompanied by numerous Scottish Lords, Marie embarked at Newhaven on 7th September. The journey took some twelve days in total and was beset by storms. Arriving in Normandy on 19th September, she was reunited with her son, Francois, Duke of Longueville, who was now fourteen. Six days later, she was greeted by Henri II and the French court at Rouen. Her daughter, Mary, Queen of Scots, aged seven, had prepared a solemn speech of welcome, but Marie brushed aside ceremony and ran towards her daughter to hug and kiss her before any speeches could be delivered.

The next few months were a combination of ceremony and politicking, as well as family reunion. According to Sir John Mason, English Ambassador at the French court, the Scots nobles spent a good deal of time arguing amongst themselves, and generally comporting themselves in such a way as to embarrass Marie. However, his reports are not necessarily entirely impartial.

Marie was reunited with her son, only to lose him. He died at Amiens in April 1551.

Giving an insight into domestic life, and demonstrating that human emotions remain much the same through the ages, there is a letter from Joan, Queen of Navarre to Marie, saying that she has heard of the alarming state of health of Marie's son, and sends to know the truth and also of Marie's health. She adds that she and her husband (Marie's cousin) will do whatever they can to help Marie. Queen Joan was one of the strongest adherents of the Huguenots in France, although they were not quite yet a faction, but family ties still mattered.

According to the aforementioned Mason, Marie outwore her welcome 'The Dowager of Scotland maketh all this court weary from the high to the low, such a beggar she is for herself. The King (Henri II) would fain be rid of her.' Mason believed the delay was caused by Marie's desire to have the arrears of the pension due to her from France under the terms of her marriage treaty paid over, whilst Henri, short of cash, was promising to send her the funds later.

There was no obvious reason for Marie to return to Scotland at all. She was not Regent, and her family were all in France. However, the Scottish Lords requested her to return to *'for the execution of justice and the ordouring of the cuntrye'*. Putting her duty to her daughter, her dynasty and her adopted country before her own pleasure, Marie agreed to return.

In October 1551, therefore, Marie embarked at Dieppe to return to Scotland. Her initial intent had been to return directly by sea, but, driven off course by storms, she took refuge at Portsmouth and sent word to Edward VI that she would take advantage of the safe-conduct that had been renewed to travel overland. A reception was organised for her at Hampton Court. A message was dispatched to the King's sisters, the Ladies Mary and Elizabeth, as well as other members of the court to invite them to meet Marie.

Marie was treated as an honoured guest by Edward VI, and the Lord President of the Council, who, now promoted to the title of Duke of Northumberland, was the same Lord Lisle who had refrained from pressing military advantage against the Scots after the death of James V. The chief hostess was Lady Margaret Douglas, Countess of Lennox, half-sister of James V and the woman Lennox had married when disappointed of Marie herself. The Lennoxes were not in good odour at Edward's court, as they failed to embrace the Protestant revolution he was embracing but Court etiquette demanded a suitable show, and for some unknown reason, despite the invitation, the Lady Mary was not present.

Whilst Marie was in England she heard that John Knox, the follower of Wishart, had served his term in the French galleys and been freed. Scenting danger, although she cannot have imagined how great a threat he eventually was to become, she sent an urgent message to her brother, Rene, the Duke of Elbouef, to capture Knox. Elbouef failed and Knox headed for Switzerland where he became even more radical in his views after coming under the influence of John Calvin. By the end of November, Marie was back in Scotland.

On her return to Scotland, Marie appears to have acted in concert with Arran, travelling with him to administer justice throughout the realm. During 1552, Arran and Marie worked together to agree the Anglo-Scots border with the English government. In August of that year, a French adjudicator confirmed his decision, which was illustrated on a map prepared by Marie and Arran.

When Mary I acceded to the throne of England, Marie corresponded with the new Queen in regard to 'disorders' and 'slaughters' on the Border, committed by the English and not redressed. Mary I, whilst pointing out that the reports she had received 'declared [the situation] to be otherwise', but that to show her 'plain affection to amity' she would appoint councillors to meet with Marie's own to resolve matters.

Chapter 8: Regent of Scotland

Following Mary's eleventh birthday on 8th December, 1553, Henri II declared that she was of age – probably rather before the Regent Arran was anticipating such a move. The age of majority for a monarch usually being somewhere above fourteen, although there was no fixed rule. In accordance with the Treaty of Haddington, therefore Arran was no longer to be Regent on the former basis of being Mary's heir and the *second person in the kingdom'*.

There would, of course, need to be someone exercising authority and as Mary was now considered of age, she was free to appoint whomever she liked – or rather, whomever Henri II liked. Queen Mary's choice, unsurprisingly, was Marie of Guise. The decision was accepted with mixed feelings, although by no means general hostility. The Scots could be sure that Marie would not have any designs on the throne herself, as Arran and Lennox were suspected of harbouring, and she had proven herself a capable member of the council prior to this date. The rub, of course, was the very thing that made her Henri's nominee – her strong allegiance to France. Her continued Catholicism did not pose an immediate problem. The majority of the Lords were still Catholic, although the Protestant group was gaining momentum.

The Court processed to Edinburgh where Arran, now Duke of Chatelherault, formally gave up his powers as Regent, and Marie was installed. In a gesture of supreme tactlessness, Marie had the crown of Scotland placed on her head by the French Ambassador d'Oisel, in theory representing her daughter, Mary, Queen of Scots, but looking very much to the entire country that the Scottish crown was in the hands of the French. Had they resisted England only to fall prey to the French?

Now Queen Mary was declared to be of age, Marie was pressed by her brother Charles, Cardinal of Lorraine, to send money for her to have her own household as Queen of Scots, rather than sharing that of the French princesses. Marie, always strapped for cash, managed this by assigning the pension of 20,000 livres she received from the French king herself, and sending some 25,000 livres from her dower estates in Scotland, as well as a further contribution from her Longueville dower.

This was despite Marie's own money troubles. There are several letters to the steward of her Ross lands, the Countess of Moray, asking the Countess to '*mak gud and haiste payment*'. She was also constrained to borrow small sums, including 200 crowns from the Countess of Montrose.

The Scottish economy still largely operated in kind and there was little actual coinage, which inhibited trade. Problems were exacerbated by the circulation of debased foreign coins. Thus, although monarchs and nobles could live well off the produce of their lands, finding large amounts of cash was difficult and made cash pensions (for which the modern mind, although not the contemporary one, might read bribes) from France and England was always an important factor in allegiance.

In part to remedy the lack of money for running the Government, in 1556 Marie requested the Estates to grant a perpetual yearly tax. This would have necessitated an inventory to be taken of every man's '*estate and substance*'. However, the Lords rejected the demand, stating that they '*meant not to putt their goodes in inventory, as if they were to make their last willes and testamentes.*'

Marie's regency saw the stepping up of hostilities between France and the empire again. South of the border, Mary I, who became queen in July 1553, immediately made moves to bring England and the Empire back into alliance, through her marriage to the Emperor's son, later Philip II of Spain. This put pressure on France, Henri II believing, not without reason, that England would join in any conflict on the Imperial side. Scotland too, would be threatened by an Anglo-Imperial alliance and a strong French presence in Scotland seemed more important than ever.

Henri's fears were confirmed when England followed Spain into war with France in June 1557. To strengthen his position, the marriage between Mary, Queen of Scots and his son Francois, took place on 24th April 1558. With the agreement of the Scottish Estates, Francois was granted the '*Crown Matrimonial*', that is, he was joint sovereign with Mary and in the event of her death would remain King. As evidence that

Scotland was under the '*protection*' of France, and not in any way a vassal state, following the wedding, the two governments granted mutual citizenship to all French and Scots.

Chapter 9: Rebellion (1557 – 1560)

Despite the marriage between Mary, Queen of Scots and the Dauphin having been planned since 1548, there was a group of Scots nobles who, by the end of December 1557, no longer wanted it to take place. The Earls of Argyll, Glencairn and Morton, with other lords signed a '*Covenant*' to bring Scotland to Protestantism. They, together with Lord James Stewart (James V's illegitimate son) invited John Knox to return from Geneva, although they then seem to have thought better of it – he received a letter when he was about to embark at Normandy, withdrawing the invitation. Knox saw their '*inconstancy*' as an affront to God, and set sail anyway.

Up until this point there had been a tacit acceptance of private Protestant preaching and some services being held in Scots. However, this was not enough for the radicals.

Marie, temperamentally inclined to tolerance, strove to preserve a balance between the Reformers and the Catholics but this became harder as the battle lines between Catholics and Huguenots became increasingly demarcated in France, and a new Protestant regime was in place in England, the Catholic Mary I having been replaced by Protestant (although not Calvinist) Elizabeth. Forced to choose, Marie issued orders for the proper Catholic observance of Easter 1559 and for all Scots to return to the old faith.

John Knox's return made compromise impossible. Knox was undoubtedly a hugely talented and charismatic preacher and writer, and although his style of preaching fire and brimstone seems excessive to modern readers, he was soon winning converts both at Court and elsewhere. His brand of Biblical fundamentalism led him to believe, and preach, that for women to '*bear rule*' was an '*abomination*' and an affront to God. He shared these views in his '*First Blast of the Trumpet against the Monstruous Regiment of Women*', published in 1558 in Geneva, which inveighed in most intemperate language against both Marie and Mary of England.

On 11th May, 1559, in direct contravention of the law, Knox preached at Perth. His sermon was so inflammatory that a member of the congregation threw a stone at a priest, and whole-scale rioting followed. Such disobedience could not be tolerated and Marie headed for Perth with troops to restore order. The Lords of the Congregation, however, supported Knox, and faced with a larger force, Marie retreated to Dunbar.

The Lords advanced on Edinburgh, arriving early in the morning of 30th June 1559. Their plan, according to Kirkcaldy of Grange, a Protestant chronicler, was to '*maintain true religion, and resist the King of France.*'

The people of Edinburgh were not notably enthusiastic at the arrival of the Lords, and in July Marie was able to drive them out and begin fortifying Leith. Of necessity, she called on French troops and their brutal behaviour alienated the Scots further.

On 21st October 1559 the Act of Suspension passed by the Lords of the Congregation to remove Marie from the Regency because, according to Knox, of her

'Interprysed destruction of thair said commounweall and overthrow of the libertie of thair native countrie.'

Marie maintained that the rebellion was against lawful authority and was not religiously motivated. The Protestants, however, did not necessarily see it the same way and they requested help from Protestant England, against Catholic domination in the same way that, nearly twenty years earlier they had requested French help against English domination.

In November 1559, the Lords of the Congregation wrote instructions to William Maitland of Lethington to carry messages to Elizabeth. He was to inform her of the *'cruelty and tyranny of the French captains and soldiers'* and the indifference of Marie to their *'frequent complaints'* and her obvious desire to conquer Scotland for France.

He was also to draw attention to the risk to Elizabeth herself of the marriage between Mary and Francois and their provocation of the English monarch by promoting Queen Mary's claim to the English throne. In support of the claim they had had a seal made quartering their arms with those of England and had sent Marie a *'staffe for hir to rest upon, having graven in the toppe the said usurped armes'*.

Lethington was then to *'beseech'* Elizabeth to *'afford them her gracious protection against the French intended conquest'*. Such a step, they continued, would allow Elizabeth to please the Almighty and procure *'perpetual love'* between England and Scotland, which love was, apparently, a thing *'much desired of all Christians, saving the French only'*.

Elizabeth hesitated. She was extremely reluctant to get involved. Although events did not always allow her free reign in her decisions, her preference was nearly always to put solidarity amongst monarchs and obedience to lawful authority above religious differences. Eventually, she was persuaded – her chief minister, William Cecil, was a determined Protestant and urged the importance of defending the Lords strongly. On 26th January, 1560, English ships arrived at Leith, and, following the February Treaty of Berwick with England, English troops arrived and by March were besieging Edinburgh Castle, with Marie in inside.

In the midst of this turmoil, Marie's health broke down completely. She referred to her ailment as *'dropsy'*, and it was probably some sort of congestive heart failure that caused her to retain water. By 1st June 1560 she could neither eat nor lie down, and knowing the end was near, she sent for Moray and Arran. After begging their forgiveness for any wrong she might have done them, she died on 11th June 1560 at Edinburgh Castle with them at her side.

Her remains were embalmed and left in the Chapel of St Margaret within the Castle precincts. The Protestant Lords refused to allow a burial in Holyrood Abbey by the Catholic rites. Eventually, in March 1561, her body was taken at night and embarked at Leith for France. She was buried at the Convent of St Pierre Les Dames, where her sister, Renee, was abbess. Her monument was destroyed during the French Revolution.

*

Marie was in many ways a successful Regent. She was clever, diplomatic and shrewd, and she achieved her immediate aims of preserving her daughter's person and crown. She was described as *'a woman with a man's courage.'* Nevertheless, Marie did no, see, or, if she saw, did not accept, that times were changing. Her ambitions, as a member of a family that strove to dominate Europe, were essentially dynastic, built on the mediaeval concept of a country as the personal fiefdom of its rulers. A move towards a more nationalist concept was growing, reinforced by the increasing rhetoric of religion as a defining characteristic of a country. The perception of Marie as the tool of a foreign state whose religion had been rejected by a large proportion of the ruling class condemned her to ultimate failure.

Aspects of Marie of Guise's Life

Chapter 10: Life of a Queen Consort

Marie was married to James V of Scotland, by proxy, at her home of Chateaudun on 29th May 1538. Her *'spousing ring'* consisted of a single diamond of the value of 300 crowns. Hopefully, no-one told her that James' first wife had had a ring to the value of 1,100 crowns! The tip paid to the notary who drew up her marriage contract was also less than he had received for the king's first marriage. Whether the difference in these sums is owing to the fact that James' first wife was a king's daughter, whilst Marie was only the daughter of a duke, or whether they reflect the lower level of enthusiasm James felt for his second marriage, is unknown.

The other important pre-nuptial expense was the collection of the Papal dispensation required because James and Marie were third cousins - both being descended from Arnold, Duke of Guelders (1410 – 1473). The expense of fetching the necessary document from Rome was 200 crowns.

Once married, Marie set out almost immediately for the coast, probably embarking from Rouen, in Normandy. Her dowry had been provided jointly by the King of France, and her father, Claud, Duke of Guise, but she does not seem to have been given any cash in hand, as, whilst at Rouen, she was obliged to borrow 450 francs against her expected income as Queen of Scots.

The new Queen's trip to Scotland was an opportunity for James to have wine shipped from France, and, together with her baggage, the flotilla, consisting of three galleys, carried 18 tuns of white wine and claret. Marie's ship was named the '*Riall*' and had a specially fitted glass window for her cabin.

Used to the splendour of the court of France, Scotland probably seemed somewhat less luxurious to Marie. However, James, with the dowries he had received both for Marie and her predecessor was, for the only time in his life, flush with money. He was a generous, not to say extravagant man, and spent lavishly on jewellery, plate and cloth.

Marie was crowned as Queen of Scots on 22nd February, 1540. The peeresses were summoned to attend her, and a completely new crown and sceptre were made for her. Fashioned of thirty-five ounces of gold, the crown was set with stones. Her sceptre was made of 31 ounces of silver-gilt. The work, carried out by the King's goldsmith, John Mosman, cost £45 Scots. The crown was further aggrandised in 1541 with the addition of another 35 ounces of gold.

Some of the gold used for the royal ornaments (including a basin of an astonishing 10lb weight) was obtained from the King's own gold-mines. Expert miners had been sent by Marie's father, Claud, Duke of Guise, in the summer of 1539 to give advice on operation of the mine. They had been given an interpreter

'*ane Scottis boy that spekis Frenche to serve them quhill thai gett the langage.*'

He received fifty shillings (£2 2s) for his service of a couple of months.

Marie benefited from the gold-mine, not just for her crown, but also in receiving a gold belt of 19 ounce weight, set with a sapphire, which cost the King £20 for making.

The King and Queen had court musicians, who received liveries twice a year. There were five Italian minstrels and four players of the viols, three of them dressed in parti-coloured red and gold, and one in head-tofoot red, with a red bonnet. They were paid the princely sum of £40 Scots. The trumpeters received about half as much. The '*tabourer*' (a tabor is a type of drum), an older man called Anthony, objected to wearing livery, and received cash to buy his own outfit instead.

As well as the household officers, Marie had her own attendants, including her French pantryman (the officer in charge of bread), M. Beglatt. She also had a French Master of Horse – an important role as he would have attended the Queen whenever she rode, and helped her mount. The Queen's geldings were looked after by an army of stable-hands, led by one William Gib.

Marie herself was attended by at least seven ladies, a mixture of French and Scots women. On the marriage of any of her attendants, it was customary to give clothes and money. Joanna Gresoner (or Gresmoir), who married Robert Beaton of Creich, received a red velvet gown to the value of £108 Scots to mark her marriage. This lady's daughter, Mary, was later one of the Four Marys who were the attendants of Marie's own daughter.

To entertain the ladies there was a female fool, called Serat, who was dressed in the usual livery colours of red and yellow, with a green kirtle. There was also a jester and a Frenchwoman, Jeanne, who was a dwarf. She was dressed in a gown of light blue velvet, with a green kirtle. Rather disturbingly to modern sensibilities, sixteenth century ladies often had dwarfs in their entourages and would send them to each other as presents.

Marie herself was sumptuously dressed. On one occasion £67 10s was spent on Venetian crimson damask for fifteen ells (about 18 yards or metres) for a gown.

During the three and a half years of her married life, Marie was pregnant three times, and she had nurses, rockers and other attendants, not only for her own children, but also for her husband's illegitimate off-spring, who were brought up in the royal nurseries.

Marie's life as Queen Consort came to an abrupt end when her thirty-year old husband died, probably of dysentery, following a disastrous campaign against the English. For mourning wear, the Queen and her attendants received 246 ells (nearly 310 yards or metres) of '*Paris*' black cloth at 70s the ell, as well as Holland cloth (a type of fine linen), black velvet and white satin. She also had long black cloth saddle cloths for her horses, and the chair of her '*chariot*' was lined with black.

Chapter 11: A Family Visit

In 1548, Marie waved goodbye to her five-year-old daughter, Mary, Queen of Scots, when the little girl sailed from Dumbarton for France. She was now without any family in Scotland. It is apparent from Marie's extensive correspondence with her mother and her siblings that she was very close to her family, and missed them, as well as her son by her first marriage, François, Duke of Longueville.

In the Spring of 1550, Marie's father, Claud of Lorraine, Duke of Guise died. She wrote to her brother, now Duke of Guise, that she had lost the best father that any child had ever lost and this bereavement may have contributed to her desire to see the land of her birth and her family again.

On 23rd July 1550, Henri II of France wrote to Edward VI of England, requesting a safe-conduct for Marie to travel through King Edward's dominions, if necessary. It was unlikely that Marie planned to travel overland, but a safe-conduct was necessary in case she should be blown off-course and land at an English port, as indeed occurred on her return trip. Whether the English King and Council would have been quite so accommodating had they known that Henri was planning a grand fete to celebrate the '*liberation*' of Scotland from English forces is questionable!

On receipt of the safe-conduct, Henri sent six galleys under the command of Pietro Strozzi, Prior of Capua, to fetch Marie. When she heard the *'joyueuse nouvelles'* of her impending visit, Marie's daughter, Mary Queen of Scots was overjoyed, writing to her grand-mother, Antoinette de Bourbon, that to see her mother would be *'the greatest happiness that [she] could desire in the world'.'*

Marie embarked on the 6th or 7th September, at Newhaven, together with a large proportion of the Scottish court, no doubt to keep as many of them close to her as possible, and also as an opportunity for Henri II to meet them and *'reward'* the supporters of the Franco-Scots alliance personally. They landed in Normandy some twelve days later, either at Dieppe or at Havre-de-Grace – the sources conflict. It is likely that Marie spent the first few days at her son's home in Normandy before travelling on to Rouen by 25th September.

The entire French Court was assembled to meet the Scottish entourage – Henri II, his wife, Catherine di Medici and their children, his influential mistress, Diane de Poitiers, and, of course, the seven year old Mary, Queen of Scots. The little Queen of Scots had been taught a formal speech to deliver to her mother, but, unusually, Marie abandoned all protocol and ran towards her little girl, scooping her up in her arms.

The court remained at Rouen for some days. A procession had been arranged, reminiscent of the triumphs of Roman generals, with the court watching from pavilions erected by the bridge over the Seine. An endless stream of officials, courtiers and actors dressed in green, blue, and white velvet and satin passed by, enacting tableaux of ancient heroes. Even a mock sea-battle was staged, although it ended badly, with some of the actors being killed when the cannon went off. According to the English envoy, Sir John Mason, there was a good deal of squabbling amongst the Scots nobles in regard to lodgings.

Marie stayed in France for over a year – travelling to her childhood home at Joinville and around the north of France. According to the English envoy, she was treated *'like a goddess'*. Henri II also feted and lavishly rewarded her Scottish nobles – tying them to the Franco-Scottish alliance with chains of gold.

Whilst Marie was in France she was deeply distressed by the discovery of an assassination plot against Mary, Queen of Scots. Following the murder of Cardinal Beaton in 1548, the holders of the fortress of St Andrew's, referred to as the *'castilians'* remained under siege for months before the castle was captured and the castilians sent to the galleys. One of these castilians, after being released, changed his name and talked his way into the Scottish Guard at the court of France. From this position, he plotted the assassination of Queen Mary in April of 1551. The plan was to poison her favourite pudding of pears. Fortunately, the plot was discovered, but Marie was so distraught she became ill.

She was sufficiently recovered by June to attend the ceremony surrounding the investiture of Henri II with the Order of the Garter. The Marquess of Northampton (William Parr, brother of Queen Katherine Parr) led the embassy at the event which took place at Chateaubriand on 20th June 1551. The English embassy made a final request for the hand of the Queen of Scots for King Edward VI, but it was refused, as she was contracted to marry the Dauphin. In recompense, a marriage was agreed between King Edward and the Princess Elisabeth, Henri II's daughter.

Henri then took Northampton and the other English envoys to the chamber of Queen Catherine, where Marie and the Queen of Scots were also present. The whole company passed the evening in dancing. The following day, the King played tennis and then the court, including Marie, watched wrestling matches between English and Breton wrestlers. Once the treaty relating to the marriage of Edward VI and the Princess

Elisabeth was agreed, Henri entertained the court with a midnight picnic and deer hunt by torch-light.

Soon after, preparations began for Marie's departure, although, in the event, she remained another two months. According to the English envoy, this was because she and Henri II were wrangling about money matters. In the last month of her stay, she lost her son, the 15 year old Duke of Longueville, who died at Amiens, with Marie at his bedside. Grief-stricken, she contemplated remaining in France, but duty called her back to Scotland. She still was not named as Regent, but was requested to return to assist with the '*execution of justice*'.

Delayed by the loss of her son, Marie did not embark for Scotland until October, although she had received a second safe-conduct from England in September. Marie set out in a flotilla of ten ships, under the leadership of Baron de la Garde. Her plan was to travel directly home but the ships were blown by storms onto the English coast, and Marie took refuge in Portsmouth. The Captain of Portsmouth, Sir Richard Wingfield, immediately went to meet her to ask whether she wished to re-embark for Scotland, or travel through England. No doubt having had enough of an autumn sea-journey, Marie elected to travel overland. The local nobles went to pay their respects, and orders were received from the King's Council to the grandees of the counties between Portsmouth and London to give her appropriate hospitality.

It took Marie several days to reach London, staying at Sir Richard Wingfield's house at Southwick for two days, then at Warblington (the castle confiscated from Margaret Plantagenet, Countess of Salisbury following the Exeter Conspiracy) with dinner at the house of the Earl of Arundel, followed by a stop at Cowdray Castle in Sussex, and then Guilford where she was met by Lord William Howard, who accompanied her to Hampton Court.

A mile or so from the Palace, the Marquess of Northampton and his wife met her. She stayed at Hampton Court until the 2nd November, and spent the evening *'in dancing and pastime'* then travelled into London by barge to stay at the Bishop of London's Palace, Baynard's Castle. The Lord Mayor sent presents of veal, mutton, swine, beer, wine coals, and even a sturgeon to make her stay more pleasant.

On the 5th November, the Duke of Suffolk (Henry Grey) and the Earl of Huntingdon (Francis Hastings, the great-great-nephew of Edward IV) waited upon her. On 6th November, the ladies of the Court, led by Marie's half-sister-in-law, Lady Margaret Douglas, Countess of Lennox, and the Duchesses of Northumberland and Suffolk and the Countess of Pembroke (Anne Parr), together with some hundred noble and gentlewomen, accompanied her to court.

The sight of Lady Margaret might have been somewhat embarrassing as Lady Margaret's husband, Matthew Stuart, Earl of Lennox, had hoped to be named Regent of Scotland in place of Arran and had been a suitor to Marie when she was first widowed. Disappointed, he had changed allegiance to support the English faction against Marie's preferred French alliance.

Despite having received invitations, the King's sisters, the Ladies Mary and Elizabeth did not attend, although their reasons for absence are not recorded. The King met Marie in the entrance at Whitehall, and she was conducted to the Queen's Side of the Palace where she dined in state on the left of the King, under the Cloth of State. The room was decorated with the King's best plate – a sideboard with four shelves of gold utensils and one of six shelves of *'massy silver'*. Having recently met the young man her daughter was contracted to marry, the Dauphin François, Marie now had the opportunity to compare him with the alternative suitor – a boy of similar age.

According to the Protestant John Knox, who was one of Edward VI's chaplains and treated him as a Protestant hero, Marie said that '*she found more wisdom and solid judgement in the young King of England than she should have looked for in any three princes of full age then in Europe.*' After dinner, which finished at around 4pm, Marie returned to the Bishop's Palace, where she rested for another day, before departing for the North. Before she left, Northumberland, Winchester and other lords paid her a final visit to present her with two horses (or nags, as they were referred to) and a ring with a diamond, presents from the King.

Messages were sent to all of the Sheriffs in the counties she would pass through to meet her and pay her the appropriate honours. She was accompanied on her journey by Edward Dudley, son of the Duke of Northumberland, and a Mr Shelley, to make sure she was '*conveniently and honourably served*'. Marie was back in Scotland before the end of November. She would not leave the country again.

Chapter 12: Following the Footsteps of Marie of Guise

The numbers against the places correspond to those on the map at the end of this article.

Marie spent her youth in France, before arriving in Scotland aged about twenty-three. During her time as Queen Consort and later Queen Dowager and Regent of Scotland, she spent the majority of her time in the central belt of Scotland, in the castles and palaces within a few days' ride of Edinburgh.

*

Marie was born in Bar (now Bar-le-Duc) a town now in the north-east of France, in the department of Meuse, but at the time of Marie's birth in 1515 in the Imperial Duchy of Lorraine. Her early childhood was spent in the Guise chateau at Joinville, which her father extended after Marie's first marriage, with the construction of the recently restored Chateau du Grand Jardin.

Marie then spent some years at the convent of the Poor Clares in Pont-a-Mousson, before returning to Bar to the household of her uncle, Antoine, Duke of Lorraine, and his wife, Renee of Bourbon-Montpensier, in about 1529.

In 1534, she joined the French Court and would have spent time at the Louvre, and in Francois I's superb chateaux, including Fontainebleu, Amboise and Chambord.

After her first marriage, which took place at the Louvre, Marie moved to her husband's lands which were centred on Amiens, where her first son was born. Her favourite home seems to have been the Chateau of Chateaudun, at the northern end of the Loire, which had been largely rebuilt by her husband's father. Marie was again in Paris, at Notre-Dame on 1st January 1537, for the marriage of the Princess Madeleine to James V of Scotland, but returned to Chateaudun to await the birth of her second child.

Marie was at Chateaudun when she heard of the death of her husband, Louis, Duke of Longueville, at Rouen and it was there that she married James V of Scotland by proxy on 29th May 1538.

Marie was more fortunate than many royal brides in that she had at least met her husband previously, and also that he was only three years older than herself, and considered to be good looking. Nevertheless, it must have been with some trepidation that she embarked from Normandy to take the rough passage through the Channel and the North Sea to Scotland. Her passage was quick and she sailed into the Firth of Forth, arriving on 10th June 1538 at Balcomie Castle, property of the Learmonth family. (1) The current building is a later replacement, dating from the second half of the sixteenth century.

On the 20th of the month, Marie and James were married at the cathedral of St Andrew's (2), the seat of the Archbishop of St Andrew's, primate of Scotland. Ancient St Andrew's, too, is gone, with only the ruins of the once vast cathedral visible.

After some months, Marie and James arrived in Edinburgh. When in the capital they divided their time between the ancient fortress of Edinburgh Castle (3) which still towers over the city from the rocky eminence of The Mound, and the new palace at Holyrood (4). Holyrood was largely created by James V and his predecessor, James IV. It was in the renaissance style, heavily influenced by French chateaux and likely to have been far more comfortable for the new Queen than the mediaeval castle. Holyrood Palace is still the official residence of HM The Queen when she is in Scotland, and is well worth a visit. The Castle is also open to tourists and displays the Honours of Scotland, as the Crown Jewels of the country are called. The crown on display is the one remodelled for James V that he wore for the coronation of Marie on 22nd February 1539.

Marie's dower included several palaces and castles. One of her personal favourites was Falkland Palace (5). Originally a hunting box, Falkland was turned into a renaissance palace by James IV and James V, with all of the most modern improvements seen in France, including a court for real tennis. During her married life, significant building works were undertaken in which Marie took a keen interest, apparently climbing a ladder to inspect works personally before authorising payment.

Another of Marie's dower castles was Linlithgow (6) and it was here that she gave birth to her third child, the only one to survive. Apparently, when asked what she thought about Linlithgow, she said she *'had never seen a more princely palace.'*

Stirling Castle (7), situated in the heart of Lowland Scotland, was probably the place where Marie spent most time. She retreated there with her daughter, the young Mary, Queen of Scots, after the death of James V, when it was feared that the little Queen would be kidnapped by the English who wanted to arrange a marriage between her and Edward, son of Henry VIII. James V had begun a new palace block within the castle walls, in the renaissance style. This has now been restored to look as it did during Marie's regency. The colours are surprisingly bright!

The Scottish Estates, having declined the offer of a match with Prince Edward of England, agreed the Treaty of Haddington. This was signed in Haddington Priory (8) on 7th July 1548, with Marie in attendance.

There were still fears for the young Queen, so Marie took her further inland from Stirling, to Inchmahome Priory (9) and then to Dumbarton Castle (10), the oldest and probably the most impregnable fortress in the whole of Scotland. There is little left of the sixteenth century structure, most of the extant building dating from some 200 years later.

As part of the Treaty of Haddington, Dunbar Castle (11) was handed over to the French. Marie was later forced to retreat there when the Lords of the Congregation rose against her in the summer of 1559.

During the War of the Rough Wooing (1543 – 1551) the English built or fortified a number of strongholds, including Broughty Castle (12). Marie and the Scottish nobles held a conference at Stirling at which they agreed that French troops would be requested to recapture Broughty. Marie watched the successful attack from the opposite bank of the River Tay, following which the English garrison surrendered the castle on 12th February 1550.

One of the duties of a Scottish monarch that Marie fulfilled as Regent for her daughter was the personal dispensing of justice. She and her court would travel to towns outside the capital where 'justices ayre' were held. Jedburgh (13), a border town which had suffered badly during the Wars of the Rough Wooing, was one of the places where Marie carried out this function.

In 1559, Marie came into conflict with the increasingly Protestant nobility. Religious tensions in Perth (15) spilled over into violence, and Marie did not have sufficient troops to impose order. Her opponents, the Lords of the Congregation, were increasingly disaffected by the French domination of Marie's government. The rebels took control of Edinburgh, but Marie had enough support for them to have to withdraw. A truce was agreed in the Articles of Leith (14), signed on 25th August 1559, which granted freedom to worship in private, according to conscience.

Marie's health was deteriorating. She took to her bed in Edinburgh Castle in early June, and died there on 11th June. Her body lay in St Margaret's Chapel, within the Castle precincts before being shipped back to France in 1561, to be buried in the Convent of St Pierre-les-Dames, in Rheims, where her sister, Renee, was abbess.

Key to Map

1.   Balcomie Castle, Fife
2.   St Andrew's Cathedral
3.   Edinburgh Castle
4.   Holyrood Palace, Edinburgh
5.   Falkland Palace, Fife
6.   Linlithgow Palace, West Lothian
7.   Stirling Castle
8.   Haddington Priory
9.   Inchmahome Priory
10.   Dumbarton Castle
11.   Dunbar Castle
12.   Broughty Castle
13.   Jedburgh Abbey
14.   Leith, Edinburgh
15.   Perth

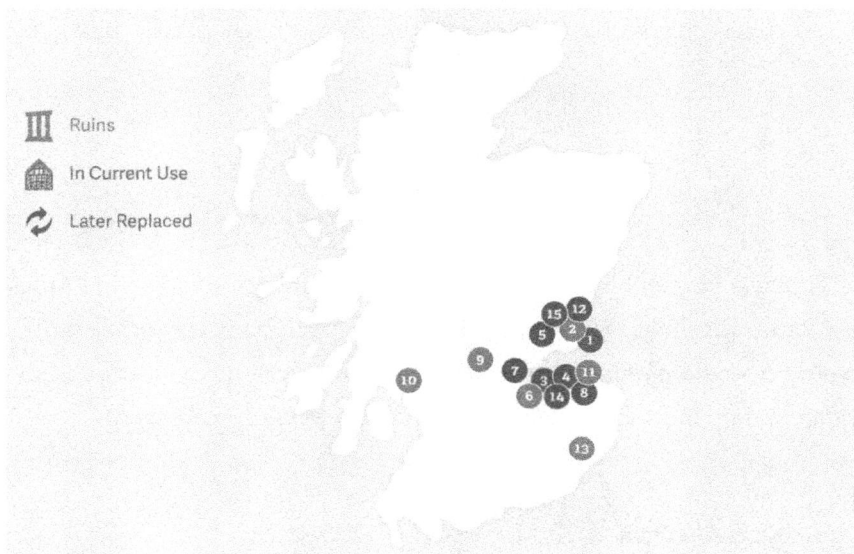

Chapter13: Two Book Reviews

The best known biographies of Marie of Guise are by Rosalind Miles and Pamela Ritchie. Unfortunately, neither of these is easy to come by, so our reviews are of books relating to her daughter Mary Queen of Scots' life and reign, in which Marie played an important part as Regent.

My Heart is My Own

Author: John Guy

Publisher: Harper Perennial UK

In a nutshell A compelling interpretation of Mary, Queen of Scots' character and motivations. Guy has put the central drama of Mary's life – the murder of Darnley – into its political context and gives a very credible theory as to the truth of events.

John Guy is an experienced and well-respected historian who has written on topics as diverse as Thomas Becket and Henry VIII's children. His academic credentials, however, have not damaged his ability to write a clear narrative of events – something that is very necessary in the extremely complex political world that surrounded Mary, Queen of Scots.

Mary has been a controversial figure from the time of her second marriage, and given her obvious intelligence and charisma, it has always been hard to understand how she could have acted in ways that, in retrospect, appear to be completely lacking in the most basic common sense, let alone political skill. By using, wherever possible, the contemporary letters and papers Guy demonstrates that most (if not all) of Mary's actions were logical and understandable within the context of the information she had available. For what comes across very clearly, is that Mary did not always have the facts in her possession that would have enabled her to make different choices.

In so far as history books have villains, then William Cecil, Secretary of State to Queen Elizabeth I of England, is, in this book, a villain of the deepest hue. In Guy's interpretation, his constant interference in Scottish politics and his unshakeable enmity towards the Catholic Queen whom he saw as a threat to a Protestant succession in England destabilised an already unstable Scottish court. Guy is also very scathing of the part that Queen Mary's Guise relatives played. Her devotion to them, and her trust in their advice are shown to be misplaced – they cared far more for their own aggrandisement in France than for their niece in faraway Scotland, although they never hesitated to use her for their own ends.

Guy is clearly sympathetic to Mary, but he cannot avoid the judgement that she threw her crown away when she became entangled with Bothwell. His interpretation is that, although her abduction was forced, she was not raped, and that she married Bothwell willingly. This is a different interpretation from that of Porter, in 'Crown of Thistles' (see page 384) and a comparison of both books is valuable.

Guy's review of the investigation into the murder of Darnley, and the Casket Letters is extremely detailed and gives a very welcome analysis of the actual evidence against the Queen – he also shows how and why it may have been fabricated.

Similarly, he gives a coherent and structured narrative of the various political imperatives that Mary was subjected to once she was imprisoned in England, and how, eventually, Mary had no choice but to support plots against Elizabeth, if she were to have any hope of regaining her freedom.

All in all, this is an excellent retelling of a well-known, but complex, story that has invited blind partisanship from many authors. Guy is clearly a supporter of Mary, and inevitably gives a positive interpretation of events where motivations are in question, but where Mary's actions were obviously wrong or foolish, he does not hesitate to say so.

Bibliography

The works listed below were consulted for several of the Profiles with more specific works related to the individuals listed under their names.

Accounts of the Treasurer of Scotland: v. 5-8:. Edinburgh: H.M. General Register House, 1877

Calendar of Border Papers: Volume 1, 1560-95 <http://www.british-history.ac.uk/cal-border-papers/vol1/> [accessed 12 November 2015]

Calendar of State Papers: Scotland <http://www.british-history.ac.uk/cal-state-papers/scotland> [accessed 10 November 2015]

Calendar of State Papers: Domestic Series: Edward VI, 1547-1553. United Kingdom: Stationery Office Books.

Calendar of State Papers: Domestic: Mary I 1553-1558. London: Public Record Office.

Calendar of State Papers Simancas, British History Online (HMSO, 1892) Hume, Martin A S, ed.,

Calendar of State Papers: Venice <http://www.british-history.ac.uk/cal-state-papers/venice/vol2/vii-lxi> [accessed 7 October 2015]

Charters and Documents Relating to the City of Glasgow 1175 - 1649, British History Online <http://www.british-history.ac.uk/glasgow-charters/1175-1649/no2/pp79-87> [accessed 17 September 2015]

Cecil Papers, http://www.british-history.ac.uk/cal-cecil-papers (Accessed: 7 September 2015)

Letters and Papers, Foreign and Domestic, of the Reign of Henry VIII:
Preserved in the Public Record Office, the British Museum, and
Elsewhere in England (United Kingdom: British History Online, 2014)
https://www.british-history.ac.uk/letters-papers-hen8/ Brewer, John
Sherren, and James Gairdner,

Coltman, Dayle, and Gordon Donaldso:, *The Edinburgh History of*
Scotland: James V-James VII v. 3 (The Edinburgh History of Scotland)
(Edinburgh: Hyperion Books, 1998)

De Lisle, Leanda, *Tudor: The Family Story* (United Kingdom: Chatto &
Windus, 2013)

De Nicolay, Nicolas: *The Navigation of James V Round Scotland, the*
Orkney Isles and the Hebrides or Western Isles

Drummond, William, ed., *The History of Scotland from the Year 1423*
until the Year 1542, Containing the Lives and Reigns of James I, II, III,
IV and V (London: H Hills for R Tomlins and himself, 1655)

Ellis, Henry, *Original Letters, Illustrative of English History: Including*
Numerous Royal Letters: From Autographs in the British Museum, the
State Paper Office, and One or Two Other Collections., 1st edn (New
York: Printed for Harding, Triphook, & Lepard, 1824)

Foxe, John, *The Acts and Monuments of John Foxe: A New and*
Complete Edition: With a Preliminary Dissertation by the Rev. George
Townsend (London: R.R. Seeley and W. Burnside, 1837)

Fraser, Antonia, *Mary Queen of Scots* (London: HarperCollins
Publishers, 1970)

Gibb, George Duncan: *The Life and Times of Robert Gib. Lord of*
Caribber, Famililar Servitor and Master of the Stable to King James V
of Scotland (London: Longmans, Green & Co., 1874)

Guy, J. (2004) *My Heart is My Own: the Life of Mary Queen of Scots*. London: Harper Perennial.

Holinshed, Raphael, *Holinshed's Chronicles of England, Scotland & Ireland* (United Kingdom: AMS Press, 1997)

Hotle, Patrick C.: *Thorns and Thistles: Diplomacy between Henry VIII and James V, 1528-1542* (Lanham, MD: University Press of America, 1996)

Keith, Robert: *History of the Affairs of Church and State in Scotland from the Beginning of the Reformation to the Year 1568* (Edinburgh: Spottiswoode, 1844),

Knox, John, *The Works of John Knox* Vols 1 - 6, ed. by David Laing (United Kingdom: James Thin, 1895)

Lang, Andrew, *The History of Scotland from the Roman Occupation: Vol III C. 79 - 1545*, 3rd edn (New York: Dodd, Mead & Co., 1903)

Lemon, Robert, ed., *Calendar of State Papers: Domestic Series: Edward, Mary and Elizabeth,* British History Online (London: HMSO, 1856)

Leslie, John, *The History of Scotland: From the Death of King James I, in the Year 1436 to 1561* (United States: Kessinger Publishing, 2007)

Lindsay of Pitscottie, Robert, *Pitscottie's Chronicles of Scotland*, ed. by Ae. J. G Mackay (Edinburgh: Blackwood for the Society, 1911)

Marshall, Rosalind K, *John Knox* (Edinburgh: Birlinn, 2008)

Marshall, Rosalind. K. (2003) *Scottish Queens 1034 - 1714*. United Kingdom: Tuckwell Press.

Marshall, Rosalind K, *Queen Mary's Women: Female Relatives, Servants, Friends and Enemies of Mary, Queen of Scots* (Edinburgh: John Donald Publishers, 2006)

Melville, James Sir and Donaldson, Gordon (ed), *The Memoirs of Sir James Melville of Halhill, Containing an Impartial Account of the Most Remarkable Affairs of State during the Sixteenth Century Not Mentioned by Other Historians, More Particularly Relating to the Kingdoms of England and Scotland under the reigns of Queen Elizabeth, Mary Queen of Scots and King James* (London: Folio Society, 1969)

Oliver, Neil: *A History of Scotland* (Phoenix PR, 2011)

Pitcairn, Robert: *Criminal Trials in Scotland from AD 1488 to AD 1624* (Edinburgh: William Tait, 1833)

Records of the Parliaments of Scotland <http://www.rps.ac.uk/> [accessed 17 September 2015]

Perry, Maria, *Sisters to the King*, 2nd edn (Andre Deutsch, 2002)

Pitcairn, Robert, *Criminal Trials in Scotland from AD 1488 to AD 1624* (Edinburgh: William Tait, 1833)

Porter, Linda, *Crown of Thistles: The Fatal Inheritance of Mary Queen of Scots* (United Kingdom: Macmillan, 2013)

Reid, Stuart, *Battles of the Scottish Lowlands* (Barnsley: Pen & Sword Military, 2004)

Ritchie, P. E. (2002) *Mary of Guise in Scotland, 1548-1560: A Political Study*. United Kingdom: Tuckwell Press.

Sadler, Sir Ralph, *The State Papers and Letters of Sir Ralph Sadler in 3 Volumes*, ed. by Arthur Clifford (Edinburgh: Archibald Constable & Co., 1809)

Stedall, Robert, *The Challenge to the Crown: The Struggle for Influence in the Reign of Mary, Queen of Scots 1542 - 1567*, 1st edn (Sussex, England: Book Guild Publishing, 2012)

Strickland, Agnes: *Lives Of The Queens Of Scotland And English Princesses: Connected With The Regal Succession Of Great Britain* (Harper & Brothers, 1859), i & ii

Strype, John, Annals of the Reformation and Establishment of Religion and Other Various Occurrences in the Church of England Etc. (Oxford: Clarendon Press, 1824),

Thornton, Tim, *'Henry VIII's Progress Through Yorkshire in 1541 and Its Implications for Northern Identities', Northern History, 46* (2009), 231–44 http://dx.doi.org/10.1179/174587009x452323

www.tudortimes.co.uk

www.ingramcontent.com/pod-product-compliance
Lightning Source LLC
Chambersburg PA
CBHW020526030426
42337CB00011B/563